INTRODUCTION

The Akita is the largest and most impressive of the seven Japanese "spitz" varieties. The term "spitz" refers to a family of dogs that shares a number of common breed characteristics as well as personality traits. The most obvious similarities include the wedge-shaped head, firmly pricked triangular ears, and the curled tail that curves over the back. Spitz-type dogs are also double coated, with the harsher outer coat standing off from the body. Further, these breeds are known to be independent and intelligent as well as somewhat stubborn.

The Akita is the largest and the most impressive of the seven Japanese spitz varieties.

Many spitz breeds are Nordic in origin and are present in a multitude of countries. It is thought that most spitz types are original breeds rather than those that were later developed by man. Unlike the mastiff-type dogs, which slowly emerged as distinctive breeds according to the work they performed, the spitz breeds have changed little over the years.

The Japanese spitz breeds, as a subdivision of this group, are all similar in appearance. The distinguishing characteristics that separate one breed from another are height and color. From the small Shiba Inu to the large Akita, one follows another according to ever-increasing height. Also, each breed has an established set of acceptable colors. While some colors overlap from breed to breed, others are more breed specific. For example, while white is acceptable in the Akita, in the Shiba Inu it is less than desirable and has caused many a debate amongst owners and breeders alike.

Finally, while the Akita shares many, if not most, of the

Representing the smallest of Japanese dog breeds, this lovely Shiba Inu is Maikohime of Akatani. "Kabuki" is owned by Andrew De Prisco.

typical spitz characteristics, there are some substantial differences that set him apart. The Akita is not as well angulated as some other of the spitz breeds and has a gait that is distinctive in the working breed ring. Also, the early Akitas had a natural dominance that created an aura of power and authority. While this temperament has been somewhat softened over the years, the breed still stands out amongst its peers.

Thus it can be said that the Akita is a spitz with an Oriental twist that makes him both attractive and compelling to the prospective owner.

Although the Japanese spitz breeds are similar in appearance, each has its own set of acceptable colors. Solid white, for example, is acceptable for the Akita while it is most undesirable for the Shiba Inu.

HISTORY

While the origin of the Akita is not precisely known, the presence of domesticated dogs used for hunting and protection dates back to the Stone Age. Though undifferentiated as to note that Korea has several native breeds that are similar in type to the Japanese breeds. The Korean Jindo is almost identical to the Japanese Shiba Inu, and the Korean Chindo-Kay is much

Korea has several native breeds that are similar in type to the Japanese breeds, such as this Jindo owned by Ted and Judy Rabinowitz.

type, the subsequent Bronze Age of Yayoi produced drawings and artifacts showing a dog with erect ears and a half-curled tail. Then, during the reign of Emperor Jimmu (600 BC.), other dogs were brought in from China and Korea. It is interesting to like the Japanese Kishu.

Due to the addition of foreign breeds, dogs present in highly populated areas were often interbred and the purity of the native breeds diminished. However, the dogs that dwelt in the more remote regions of the country were able to maintain their purity simply through the lack of contact with other breeds. However, this seclusion later created more serious problems whereby many of the native Japanese breeds faced potential extinction at various times in their history.

Initially, Japanese dogs were named for their place of origin. The designation Akita Inu was not given until 1931 when the breed was declared a natural monument. Prior to that time, the dogs from the Odate region were referred to simply as the Odate Dogs. During the feudal period of Japanese history, these dogs were called Nambu-inu or Southern Regional Dog. Dogs used for

The Akita represents an ancient Japanese breed type. The name comes from the Akita Prefecture where these dogs were originally found.

The Kishu is a member of the medium-sized division of Japanese breeds known as Shika Inus. Its most common color is solid white.

fighting were known as Kuriya-inu and those for hunting were Matagi-inu.

Regardless of the name used, it is clear that the ancestors of the Akita came from the Akita Prefecture, which is the northernmost province on the main Japanese Island of Honshu where the City of Odate is located.

Over the years, different organizations developed with the goal of preserving and/or restoring the Akita. During the Meiji Period (1868-1912), when dog fighting was allowed, the Enyukai Club was formed. Later, during the Taisho Period (1912-

1925), the Akita Kyokai dog fighting club came into existence. Finally, in 1927, the Akita-inu Hozonkai (AKIHO) was formed and became the largest and most dominant Akita club in modern day Japan. Two other organizations, which have their own registries and standards for the Akita, are the Nippon-ken Hozonkai (NIPPO), formed in 1928, and the Akita-inu Kyokai (AKIKYO), formed in 1948. The Japanese Kennel Club (JKC) also registers the breed and has a breed standard. However, the JKC and NIPPO are the predominant registries in Japan that are looked to and/or recognized on an international level. Only recently has the American Kennel Club accorded official recognition to the JKC as an approved foreign registry.

Prior to 1930, there are few records or pictures available from which to obtain information regarding the early specimens of the breed. However, two names appear frequently: Tochini-Go, who was owned by Mr. Isumi, the first chairman of AKIHO, and Babagoma-Go, who was owned by Mr. Kunio Ichinoseki of Odate City. These two dogs are credited with substantial influence on the early lines of Akitas. Other important dogs include Ichinoseki Goma-Go who was bred to Futatsui Goma-Go and produced Goromaru-Go, who is considered by many to be the most important dog in the effort to reestablish the breed following World War II. Despite warnings from other breeders and fanciers

that Goromaru-Go would produce the then undesirable pinto coloring and long coats, known as "Moku," he was used extensively and established an enviable reputation in and out of the show ring. Upon his death in 1956, at nine years of age, his funeral was attended by Akita fanciers from all over Japan.

The respect and dedication shown to the breed by owners, breeders, and, often, the general public is not unusual. Perhaps the best known story is the one involving the ever faithful Hachi-Ko. He was whelped in 1923 and owned by Mr. Eisaburo Uyeno of Tokyo. From January 1924 until May 1925, Hachi-Ko accompanied his master daily to the train station. The dog would see Mr. Uyeno off to the Imperial University, where he held the Chair of Professorship in the Department of Agriculture, each morning and then patiently await his return in the afternoon. When his master failed to return one afternoon, having died during the work day, Hachi-Ko continued his daily vigil until March 8, 1934, when he himself died at the Shibuya Station on the very spot he had last seen his master in May of 1925. The dog's nine-year vigil deeply touched those who had observed him as he patiently waited for a master who would never return. Thus, in commemoration of his faithfulness, a statue was commissioned in 1934. The bronze was sculpted by the famous Mr. Teru Ando and stood until 1945 when it was removed by the army and used to make weaponry. The current statue, similar in size and shape to the original, was sculpted by Mr. Takeshi Ando, son of Mr. Teru Ando who had been killed during the war. The actual dog is preserved and displayed at the

Keller discovered this magnificent breed. Blind since birth, her fascination with the Akita is indicative of the breed's presence and apparent "spiritual" qualities. During her trip to Japan in 1937, where she toured for ten weeks on the lecture circuit, she visited

五 郎 丸 号

Goromaru-Go is considered by many to be the most important dog in the effort to reestablish the breed following World War II.

Japanese Museum of Natural History in Tokyo.

Another interesting story is that of Kamikaze-Go, the first Akita to come to the United States. Long before the breed caught the eye of American military personnel during the occupation of Japan following World War II, Helen

Akita City. Knowing of her desire to own an Akita, Mr. Ichere Ogasawara, a member of the local police department, presented her with a puppy from his breeding program. This dog returned to the United States to live on Ms. Keller's New York estate. Unfortunately, he took ill and died

Since the declaration of the breed as a Natural Japanese Monument in 1931, a concerted effort on the part of breeders has produced generation after generation of Akitas that are consistent in type, conformation, and color.

later that same year. However, her love for the breed did not diminish and another dog was sent to her in 1939. Kenzan-Go lived with her until his death in 1944 or 1945.

These two events, combined with the declaration of the breed as a natural monument in September 1931, assured the Akita of continued survival as a distinctive breed. Following the designation as a natural monument, there are records of a strong surge of renewed activity designed to restore the Akita to its original state. This renewed activity, begun in the 1920s, prevented the extinction of the breed following World War II. War, in all its many forms, invariably takes its toll on people and animals. The ensuing shortages of commodities, especially food, makes survival difficult at best. Large dogs like the Akita suffer the greatest consequences in that they consume greater amounts of food that, during times of strife, are reserved for the people first. Further, shortages of other commodities during harsh weather months resulted in the use of dog and cat pelts for warmth. Again, the larger breeds suffered greater losses since their coats were larger and thicker. Only shepherds, which were used as military dogs, were actively preserved. At one point, the police department issued orders that all dogs except the shepherds be caught and destroyed. While there are no accurate records as to the actual number of Akitas that survived this period, there were 60 specimens of the breed entered in the 1948 AKIHO Show. Some of these were survivors of the wartime era.

From 1948 to 1950, many historically important Akitas were produced. Their popularity was on the upswing and the increase in numbers focused more importance on the pedigrees of the dogs. The following 30 years of concentrated effort produced an Akita that was consistent in type, conformation, and color. This was the breeders' reward for a unified vision to work toward, as well as a strong registry (AKIHO) dedicated to moving the breed forward into the future. Their ability to see the breed in a historical context as well as their dedicated reverence to a national dog sets the Japanese breeders apart from other owners and breeders. The intent is not to change but to perfect what is already there.

THE AMERICAN AKITA

Like many other breeds that are well established in their countries of origin and/or on an international basis, it is not necessarily the first specimen that enters the United States that attracts the eye of the dog fancy. Such was the case with the Akita. While Helen Keller owned two on her New York estate, it was not until the years following World War II that the breed took a foothold in America.

The primary sources of imported dogs were servicemen returning from being stationed in Occupied Japan. While both the east and west coasts saw their share of Akitas, California

Tamakumo-Go counts among the most important sires whose lines were crossed with those of Goromaru-Go. Both dogs are behind many Akitas in the United States.

received the greatest numbers and still ranks number one in the total number of breed specimens. Even though the dogs were not highly promoted by their importers, there was enough interest generated to create a market for the breed. Initially, breed growth progressed slowly. Unfortunately, there was little uniformity as to type in the early dogs and few concerted breeding programs developed.

As with any new breed, the early years are tough. This is especially true when the dogs originate in countries where a language barrier prevents an easy exchange of information. This is especially true with the Akita as the pedigrees needed translation as well. Most early Akita owners were not established dog fanciers or breeders. In many cases this was their first dog and they had little idea of how to proceed. While several organizations did form, none stayed active for long until the Akita Dog Association of America was established in 1952 by Mr. M. Kelly Spellmeyer. Then in 1956, the Akita Kennel Club

A historic win for Ch. Tobe's Return of the Jedi, his eighth and final Best of Breed win at the Westminster Kennel Club. "Ben" holds the record for most Bests in Show won by an Akita: 21! Owned by Ruth Winston, handled by Vic Capone.

Ch. O'BJ BigSon of Sachmo is the son of the breed's #1 sire, Ch. Okii Yubi's Sachmo of Makoto, ROMXP, and is himself the #3 sire. BigSon is as close as an Akita can get to the standard and is one in a line of over 200 champion O'BJ Akitas bred by America's #1 breeders Barbara J. and Bill Andrews.

was established. Subsequently, the word "kennel" was dropped and by 1959 it became the Akita Club of America. A registry was finally established, patterned after the American Kennel Club. However, life in the Akita world did not get any smoother as splinter groups broke away; people joined the other associations or formed their own, though eventually many returned to the Akita Club of America. Accusations of stud book and registration theft were raised and withdrawn over the years. Finally, the recognition of the breed in 1973 by the American Kennel Club resolved the underlying conflicts by recognizing the Akita Club of America as the official parent club for the breed in the United States.

For the Akita, it was an extremely long road to official American Kennel Club recognition. The breed was accepted into the Miscellaneous Class on July 13, 1955, which is a preliminary step that all new breeds must take before being officially recognized. The first dogs shown were at the Orange Empire Kennel Club show in San Bernadino, California on January 26, 1956. While in Miscellaneous, the parent club still registered individual dogs and awarded titles. Just prior to the breed's formal American Kennel Club

Pinto coloration is not favored by the Japanese breeders. Many pinto-colored Akitas were exported to the US, as Japanese breeders could sell their undesirable stock to naive Americans for top dollar.

recognition in 1973, the registry boasted 3,082 dogs.

The first dog entered into the Akita Club of America stud book was a male named Nikko-Go whelped on March 13, 1952. However, other than being notable as the first ever entry into the registry, he had no further impact on the breed. The first stud dog to impact the American breeding

program was Homare No Maiku-go, whelped on July 10, 1953 at the Shitara Kennel in Japan. Many of these early dogs were Japanese imports. However, that would eventually end because the American Kennel Club did not recognize a foreign registry in Japan. Once the breed received official recognition beyond the Miscellaneous Class, the stud book would be closed and the Akita breeders would be limited to what was already registered and what might be available from recognized registries of other countries. Thus, the stage was set for the eventual development of what is known as the "American Akita," which is dramatically different from the Akita native to Japan almost to the point, in some fanciers' opinions, as to constitute an entirely different breed of dog. Today, this is even more interesting in that newly imported Akitas from Japan are being seen in the show ring. Upon recognition of the Japanese Kennel Club (JKC) on April 13, 1992, the American Kennel Club finally allowed new bloodlines into the stud book. Some of these dogs have been highly successful, while others are so dramatically different from what the US fanciers and judges are used to that they are being used primarily as new breeding stock for existing dogs. However, the consistency that is available in the Akitas from Japan cannot but help to improve the American dogs. The future of the Akita in the United States is much brighter than it has been in the recent past.

Thanks to the work of responsible breeders, the future of the Akita in the United States is brighter than it has ever been.

THE BREED STANDARD

Breed standards evolve over time. This is especially true when an established breed is introduced from one country to another. Each registering organization has its own requirements as to the format, contents, and language required in the written description of the ideal specimen of the breed. The standard from the country of origin is not often in conformance with the requirements of the organization that the fanciers are applying to for recognition. Often there are sections that simply do not exist, terminology that is incompatible, and overly verbose descriptive passages. Further, in the international arena, judges have an unwritten and accepted interpretation of each standard that they all know and use. On the other hand, the American judges are quite literal. If it is not written in black and white, it simply does not exist. This has caused many an exhibitor a lot of problems over the years and has necessitated multiple revisions to

The Akita is large, powerful, and alert, with much substance and heavy bone.

new breed standards before final approval.

To understand how the Akita standard developed, one must first look to the accepted standard in Japan. The most important standard was published by the Nippon-ken Hozonkai, also known as the Society for the Preservation of Japanese Dogs. There the Japanese dogs were generically known as the Nippon Inu and the standard described first the general characteristics shared by all the dogs and then presented the particulars according to size. Thus, one standard encompassed multiple dog breeds. This is understandable in that the Japanese spitz varieties differ only as to height and color. However, it was a difficult concept for the US fanciers to grasp and has caused much confusion along the way.

Over the years, many questions regarding specific characteristics of the breed have caused repeated debate and concern and have resulted in repeated revisions of the Akita Club of America breed standard. The first breed standard, accepted by the American Kennel Club in 1960, was very general. In 1963, after much research and study, a new standard was approved that tightened and/or more

AMERICAN KENNEL CLUB STANDARD FOR THE AKITA
   General Appearance—Large, powerful, alert, with much substance and heavy bone. The broad head, forming a blunt triangle, with deep muzzle, small

The Akita's large curled tail, balancing his broad head, is characteristic of the breed.

fully detailed individual breed traits. Repeatedly the issues of size, color, and the wrinkle factor were hotly debated. However, the current standard, which was adopted on December 12, 1972, has survived all attempts at further revision.

eyes and erect ears carried forward in line with back of neck, is characteristic of the breed. The large, curled tail, balancing the broad head, is also characteristic of the breed.
   Head—Massive but in balance with body, free of wrinkle when at ease. Skull

flat between ears and broad, jaws square and powerful with minimal dewlap. Head forms a blunt triangle when viewed from above. *Fault—Narrow or snipy head.* **Muzzle**—Broad and full. Distance from nose to stop is to distance from stop to occiput as 2 is to 3. **Stop**—Well defined, but not too abrupt. A shallow furrow extends well up forehead. **Nose**—Broad and black. Liver permitted on white Akitas, but black always preferred. *Disqualification— Butterfly nose or total lack of pigmentation on nose.* **Ears**—The ears of the Akita are characteristic of the breed. They are strongly erect and small in relation to rest of head. If ear is folded forward for measuring length, tip will touch upper eye rim. Ears are triangular, slightly rounded at tip, wide at base, set wide on head but not too low, and carried slightly forward over eyes in line with back of neck. *Disqualification—Drop or broken ears.* **Eyes**—Dark brown, small, deep-set and triangular in shape. Eye rims black and tight. **Lips and Tongue**—Lips black and not pendulous; tongue pink. **Teeth**—Strong with scissors bite preferred, but level bite acceptable. *Disqualification—*

The Akita has a broad head, which forms a blunt triangle, with a deep muzzle, small eyes, and erect ears.

Noticeably undershot or overshot.
   Neck and Body—Neck—Thick and muscular; comparatively short, widening gradually toward shoulders. A pronounced crest blends in with base of skull. **Body**—Longer than high, as 10 is to 9 in males; 11 to 9 in bitches. Chest wide and deep; depth of chest is one half height of dog at shoulder. Ribs well sprung; brisket well developed. Level back with firmly-muscled loin and moderate tuck-up. Skin pliant but not loose. *Serious Faults— Light bone, rangy body.*
   Tail—Large and full, set high and carried over back or against flank in a three-quarter full, or double curl, always dipping to or below level of back. On a three-quarter curl, tip drops well down flank. Root large and strong. Tail bone reaches hock when let down. Hair coarse, straight and full, with no appearance of a plume. *Disqualification—Sickle or uncurled tail.*
   Forequarters and Hindquarters—Shoulders strong and powerful with moderate layback. Forelegs heavy-boned and straight as viewed from front. Angle of pastern 15 degrees from vertical. *Faults—Elbows in or out,*

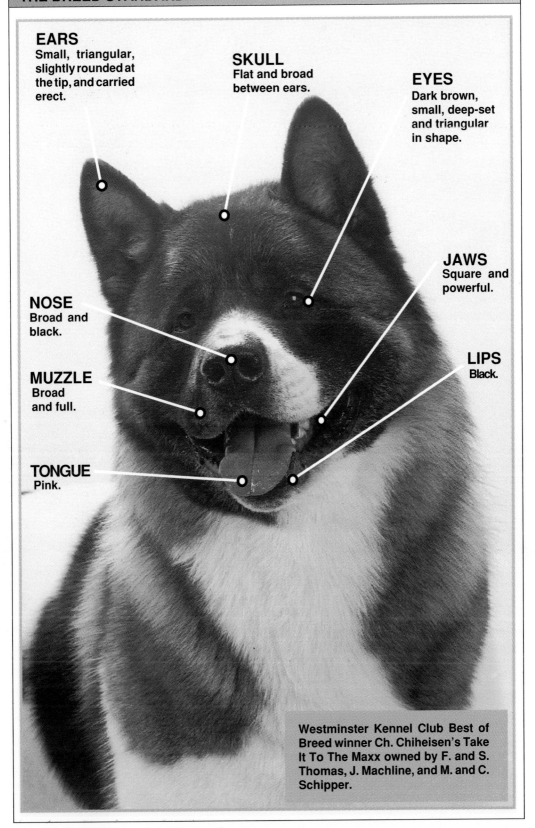

EARS
Small, triangular, slightly rounded at the tip, and carried erect.

SKULL
Flat and broad between ears.

EYES
Dark brown, small, deep-set and triangular in shape.

JAWS
Square and powerful.

NOSE
Broad and black.

LIPS
Black.

MUZZLE
Broad and full.

TONGUE
Pink.

Westminster Kennel Club Best of Breed winner Ch. Chiheisen's Take It To The Maxx owned by F. and S. Thomas, J. Machline, and M. and C. Schipper.

loose shoulders. **Hindquarters—** Width, muscular development and bone comparable to forequarters. Upper thighs well developed. Stifle moderately bent and hocks well let down, turning neither in nor out. **Dewclaws—** On front legs generally removed; dewclaws on hind legs generally removed. **Feet—** Cat feet, well knuckled up with thick pads. Feet straight ahead.

Coat— Double-coated. Undercoat thick, soft, dense and shorter than outer coat. Outer coat straight, harsh and standing somewhat off body. Hair on head, legs and ears short. Length of hair at withers and rump approximately two inches, which is slightly longer than on rest of body, except tail, where coat is longest and most profuse. *Fault—Any indication of ruff or feathering.*

Color— Any color including white, brindle or pinto. Colors are brilliant and clear and markings are well balanced, with or without mask or blaze. White Akitas have no mask. Pinto has a white background with large, evenly placed patches covering head and more than one-third of body. Undercoat may be a different color than outer coat.

Gait— Brisk and powerful with strides of moderate length. Back remains strong, firm and level. Rear legs move in line with front legs.

The Akita's gait is brisk and powerful with strides of moderate length. The back should remain strong, firm, and level.

Although the breed standard does not allow long-coated Akitas to be shown in conformation, many are bred and prove to have excellent temperaments.

Size—Males 26 to 28 inches at the withers; bitches 24 to 26 inches. *Disqualification—Dogs under 25 inches; bitches under 23 inches.*

Temperament—Alert and responsive, dignified and courageous. Aggressive toward other dogs.

DISQUALIFICATIONS

Butterfly nose or total lack of
   pigmentation on nose.
Drop or broken ears.
Noticeably undershot or
   overshot.
Sickle or uncurled tail.
Dogs under 25 inches; bitches
   under 23 inches.

ANALYSIS OF THE BREED STANDARD

The key to interpretation of the Akita standard is the concept of balance. For example, the height balances the length of the body; the tail structure and placement balances the head; and the muscularity and moderate angulation of the rear balances the shoulder layback of the front. Thus, the Akita is a total package where all the individual features must interact with each other. The dog is more than a sum of his parts.

In addition to the overall appearance of the breed, the concept of presence is an integral part of the package. The way in

A red and black brindle coat should lean toward subtle color; the rich red is not preferred. The brindle pattern always covers the body and may appear on the face.

While the temperament and dominance of the breed have been softened over the years, the Akita still has an impressive presence in the show ring.

Another important physical characteristic of the breed is color. The standard calls for colors that are "brilliant and clear." While the white coat is an exception to this rule, all other coat colors change to deeper and richer hues as the dog matures. The coat color a puppy is born with is not necessarily that which will be present in the same adult. For example, most black Akita puppies do not stay pure black.

Color has also been one of the most controversial elements of the standard. The American Kennel Club standard allows for "any

A red coat comes in many varying shades from a light orangish color to a deep, rich, almost ruby red.

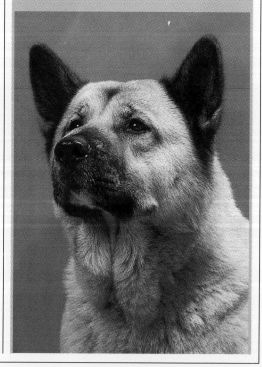

which an Akita stands, well up on his toes, the position of the head, and the set and look of the eyes all combine to convey "attitude." The Akita should impact the observer mentally and emotionally as well as visually. The Akita has what is commonly referred to as "style," which is the elegance and carriage of the dog that demonstrates those subtle extra details that give him a noble air. It is said that in the early days of Akitas, their mere presence caused a sensation ringside. As they approached the ring, their dominance was apparent when other working breeds gave way to let them pass. Spectators around the ring report feeling almost a static charge to the atmosphere.

color including white, brindle or pinto," while the Japanese standard calls for more specific colors. Allowed color is more important to the Japanese than the Americans because of the interaction of the Akita with the other six Japanese spitz varieties. However, the recognition of the Shiba Inu, the smallest of the restrictive selection favored in Japan. However, the fact that US dog fanciers and judges have already had many years of exposure to the Akita does not bode well for the restrictions being imposed on the Shiba Inu, in that many consider the Shiba to be merely a miniature version of the Akita. While this is not

Pinto coloration is defined as a white background with large evenly placed patches covering the head and more than one-third of the body.

Japanese spitz varieties, by the American Kennel Club may throw greater emphasis on color selection. The wide range of colors allowed in the Akita standard has sparked much controversy among the Shiba Inu fanciers. While some of the Shiba Inu fanciers want a wide open range of allowed colors, others prefer the more necessarily true, the impact of the one breed upon the other is unavoidable.

While the specifications for the pinto coloration of the Akita are not always easy to conform to, most of the other popular colors are relatively easy. In a white Akita, the most desired is the pure white with silver tipping.

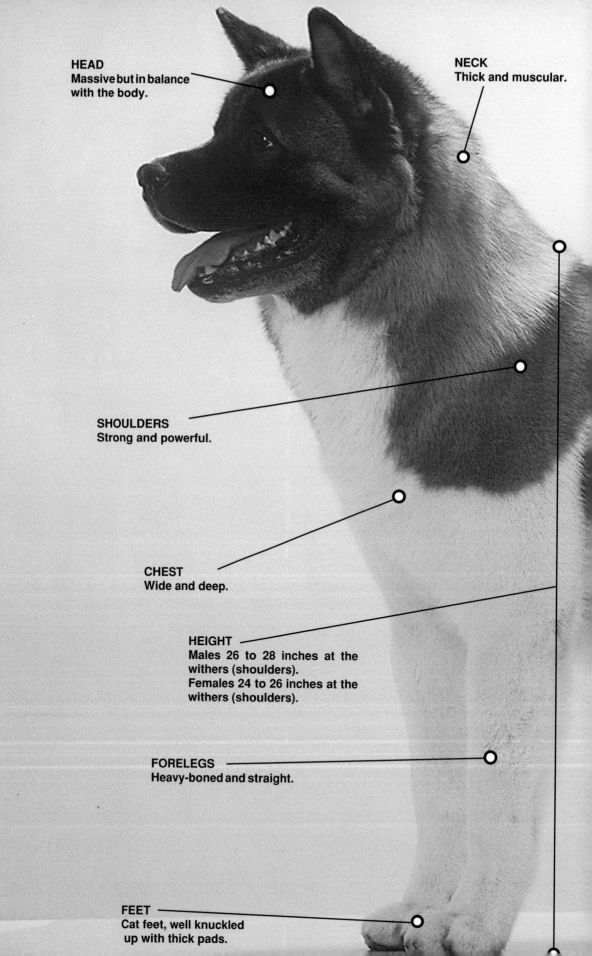

HEAD
Massive but in balance
with the body.

NECK
Thick and muscular.

SHOULDERS
Strong and powerful.

CHEST
Wide and deep.

HEIGHT
Males 26 to 28 inches at the
withers (shoulders).
Females 24 to 26 inches at the
withers (shoulders).

FORELEGS
Heavy-boned and straight.

FEET
Cat feet, well knuckled
up with thick pads.

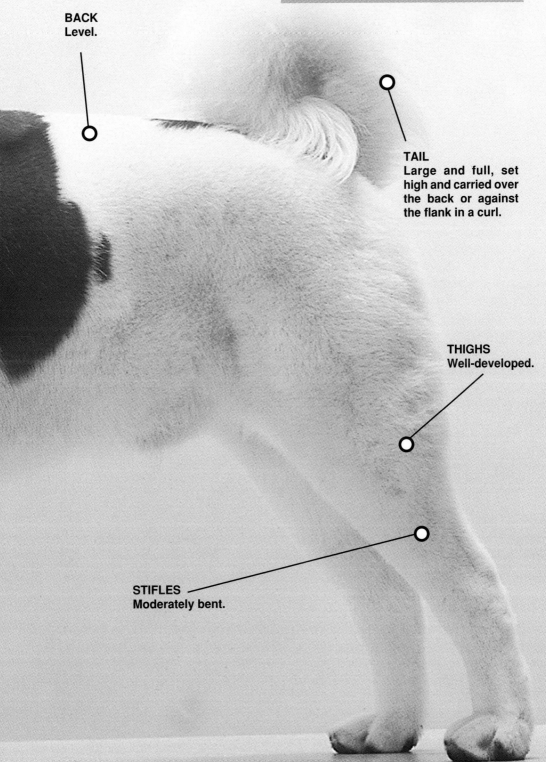

BACK
Level.

TAIL
Large and full, set high and carried over the back or against the flank in a curl.

THIGHS
Well-developed.

STIFLES
Moderately bent.

Dark eyerims and lips serve as a much desired accent. The most striking is a solid black nose; however, liver is acceptable. A red coat comes in many varying shades from a light, orangish color to a rich, deep, almost ruby red. However, the soft undercoat of a different color may change the overall visual effect. A brindle will appear in various shades of tiger striping. The "pepper and salt" brindle has a lighter shade of black with whitish coat color on the muzzle and limbs. The red and black brindle should lean toward subtle color, and the rich red is not preferred. The brindle pattern always covers the body and may appear on the face. In all but the white Akita, a white or black mask is acceptable.

While the Akita is not a "head breed," the head is important to the overall appearance of the dog. The head of the Akita is said to be a study in triangular shapes. The wedge-shaped muzzle is overlooked by triangular-shaped eye openings and capped by firmly pricked, triangular-shaped ears. Again, balance is extremely important. The head must be broad with full cheeks to offset the shapes of the accessory parts. Overly refined heads accentuate too dramatically the shape and placement of the pieces of the head and result in discord rather than the harmony of features desired. However, the size of the head is probably the most controversial subject today. The Akita in Japan has a more refined head that still imparts a sense of harmony to the features. The head of the "American" Akita is said to be overdone and bear-like.

Also distinctive to the Akita head is the deep furrow or crease down the center of the forehead. However, the slightly rounded forehead is to be free of wrinkles. The nose is large and black, except in white Akitas who can have liver-colored noses, and pretty much square in shape. The head is also indicative of sexual characteristics. The male's head is masculine and the bitch's head is feminine.

The neck is well arched and in harmony with the tail set of the dog as are the front and rear quarters of the animal. The compact, almost square form is powerful, tightly put together, and well balanced.

The concept of balance is most apparent from a judge's perspective. The eye should run smoothly from one end of the dog to the other. Should the eye stop at any one point of the dog, that feature is incorrect. A body that is too long will distort the visual impact of the front and rear quarters by moving them too far away from each other. A head that is too refined will also distort the desired balance between it and the rear/tail structure of the animal. A tail that is set too low or improperly curled will make a proper head and neck look overdone and improperly accentuate the front structure as opposed to the rear. The same will be true in the reverse.

With proper structure comes proper movement. A dog that is not correctly built simply cannot move

The head of the Akita is said to be a study in triangular shapes. The wedge-shaped muzzle is overlooked by triangular-shaped eye openings and capped by firmly pricked triangular-shaped ears.

as it should. However, the correct gait of the Akita has taken some getting used to in the Working Group classification. Most working type breeds are well angulated and have lots of reach and drive. The Akita, on the other hand, is only moderately angulated in the rear and moves with a more restricted stride. Furthermore, the rear legs move in line with the front legs. Thus the front will not have as much reach and the rear will not have as much drive as other members of the same group and while a longer backed Akita may appear, in comparison with other breeds, to have the better movement, this is not in fact true. The Akita is only slightly longer than tall and correct movement must be looked for in the properly structured dog, rather than one whose body is built to compensate for a misunderstood breed trait.

The temperament of the Akita is another often misinterpreted characteristic. As previously stated, the breed had an extremely strong presence when it first entered the

Akitas are independent and somewhat stubborn in nature; however, they want to please and will eventually conform to their owners' wishes.

United States. They were once used as fighting dogs in Japan and can be dog aggressive. However, if you understand the background of dog fighting and the role of the handler in the "pit" you will no longer assume that the breed is necessarily people aggressive. Fighting dog handlers had to be able to control their dogs in and out of the arena. Getting bitten by their own dogs was unacceptable. Further, the role of the breed as a hunter and guardian lends even greater credence to the position that the breed has an extremely stable temperament. Courage and presence do not necessarily translate into aggression. In fact, most Akitas are very sweet with people and only need to be taught good judgment in the interaction with people and society to be successful. They are highly intelligent, though somewhat independent and stubborn in nature. However, they want to please and will eventually conform to their owners' wishes and control.

Most Akitas are very sweet with people. However, as with all breeds, Akitas should not be left alone with small children.

SELECTING AN AKITA PUPPY

All puppies are cute and Akita puppies are especially so. They often look like big, woolly bear cubs. However, that puppy is going to grow into a sizable dog and you want to be careful to select the best one for your personality and lifestyle.

Akitas carry a heavy double coat. Therefore, there is a need for regular grooming. Brushing is required on a regular basis, especially during the shedding periods. Also, the puppy will grow into a large and powerful adult and as a puppy will need to be socialized and taken to some form of obedience training. He will also require consistent and firm control tempered with a loving hand. Patience is a must, these are spitz type dogs and can be somewhat independent and stubborn at times. Generally, like any puppy, an Akita will require that the new owner make a substantial commitment of time and energy. If any of these factors make you think twice about bringing an Akita into your home, you may want to reconsider your breed choice. Too many Akitas end up in pounds and with rescue groups because of hasty purchase decisions resulting in too much dog or time commitment for the owner.

When you are choosing your Akita puppy, bring the children along to help in the decision. This little girl has a tough choice to make!

If you do decide to venture into the Akita breed, the first cautionary note is not to become color blind. Just because you like the pinto pattern or are absolutely crazy about a rich, red coat does not mean that this is the ideal puppy for your home and family. Color is a purely cosmetic factor. Structure and temperament are much more important in selecting a new family member. Look for the puppy that is outgoing and friendly. Avoid the shy one and, unless you are experienced, don't gravitate to the one with the dominant attitude.

The choice of a male or female is personal preference more than anything else. The male is larger and more impressive, but takes longer to mature and will have a

Akita puppies look like cute little woolly bear cubs. Remember that they will eventually grow into sizable dogs and you must be careful to choose the best one for your lifestyle.

You want to choose a puppy that is sociable and outgoing. This Akita pup extends a friendly paw.

more difficult adolescence. The female is smaller and somewhat lighter. She will mature more quickly. However, until spayed, you will have an estrous cycle to deal with every six months or so.

Puppy coats should be full and shining with good health. While the acceptable coat is relatively short, there are long coated Akitas, also known as "woollies." They are usually heavier boned and carry a more massive head than the more traditional puppy. They are also a favorite of the pet buyer and should not be discounted as a prospect unless you are looking for show or breeding quality animals.

Finally, if possible, see the parents of the puppy. They are good indicators as to how the puppy will mature over the years.

If possible, it is a good idea to see the parents, especially the dam, of the litter you are selecting from. This will be a good indicator of how the puppies will mature.

When selecting an Akita puppy, structure and temperament are the most important factors.

CARING FOR YOUR AKITA

BRINGING UP THE AKITA BABY

The Akita puppy will require time and effort. He is intelligent and willing to please but needs to learn his limits. A good beginning is a puppy kindergarten class. This will provide the necessary socialization that the dog needs as well as a light, easy form of basic training. Also, take your puppy with you as often as possible. The more exposure he or she gets the better. Providing the person you purchased your puppy from has done their job in raising the litter properly, you have a solid foundation upon which to build.

Make sure that you are consistent with training methods and corrections. The Akita does not respond well to harsh treatment, but does want to please when the firm hand is tempered with love. Also, get the puppy used to being groomed at an early age. Many spitz-type breeds do not like to have their feet handled. It is much easier to have a wresting match with an eight-week-old puppy than an 18-month-old recalcitrant adolescent. The same is true of brushing and bathing.

The Akita puppy requires time and patience when housebreaking. Make sure that you are consistent with training methods and corrections.

The Akita is generally good natured with children and will take a lot of poking and prodding without complaint. However, there are many parts of the Akita that can be pulled at by small hands. It is therefore imperative that children of all ages be taught how to properly handle the dog whether a puppy or adult.

The Akita's ears will usually come up on their own with no help from the owner. Though some ears will droop again when the puppy is teething, they will usually come back after the teeth have been cut. Before intervening, make sure you know why the puppy is having a problem with his ears. An infection can cause the puppy to hold the ears back or down as well as changes brought on by growth spurts. Always give the ear ample time to rise of its own accord before intervening. However, occasionally the ear will is the traditional method whereby the tape is wound about the ear in the direction of the natural fold of the ear. Left on about a week, most ears will stand. However, be sure that the tape you use is air permeable to prevent irritation and infection. Another method is called the "no-tape" method whereby mole foam is cut to fit inside the ear to hold it erect. Skin bond,

The Akita's ears will usually come up on their own with no help from the owner. Though the ears may droop again while the puppy is teething, they will usually come back up after the teeth have been cut.

need assistance. Sometimes merely shaving the fur off the ear will remove sufficient weight for it to stand on its own. Once the ear is firmly erect, the hair can grow back without causing it to drop again. If all else fails, there are several methods of taping that can be used. The most common available from the local pharmacy, holds the piece in place. Again, about a week should accomplish the task. When inserting, make sure the base of the piece is well seated inside the ear so that it forms an ample platform to hold the narrower top, and thereby the ear, erect. Another method is to use a device that is placed inside the ear and then the ear is curled and taped around it. The best product is a wire curler that can be bent into the position you want for the ear. Wrap the curler in tape so that it does not irritate the inside of the ear. Then seat it well down into the base of the ear and tape the ear itself around the curler. Again, about a week should remedy the problem.

GROOMING

The Akita has a dense double coat. The undercoat is soft while the outer coat or "guard hair" is much coarser. The coat colors, in most cases, are vivid. It is important that these coat features are kept in mind when grooming the Akita.

The double coat requires regular brushing. While the coarser outer coat will shed most of the surface dirt that the dog comes into contact with on an everyday basis, it will be necessary to remove dead coat as well as any dirt that may, upon occasion, make its way into the undercoat. It is also important that all dead undercoat be removed prior to bathing or it will mat to the skin and be difficult, if not impossible, to remove. A basic pin brush is sufficient for most grooming, but during heavier shedding times a rake will make your and the dog's life easier. Remember that the male carries a heavier coat than the female and will require more frequent attention.

When preparing to give your Akita a bath, the coat color may influence your choice of shampoo. There are many good color enhancers available on the market. The coat condition may also affect your choices; however, if you are planning to show the dog, avoid cream rinses unless you can give the coat several days to return to its natural texture.

In bathing the dog, the coarse outer coat that forms a protective barrier against dirt and weather will also repel water to varying degrees. So, before pouring any shampoo on the coat, make sure that both the outer coat and undercoat are both thoroughly saturated. A spray attachment or detachable shower head are probably the best devices, as they can be worked down into the coat to more deeply concentrate the water flow. This is also true when rinsing the dog as you need to disperse the water in a way that all of the shampoo is removed from the undercoat.

Once thoroughly rinsed, you will want to towel dry the dog before allowing him to shake off the excess water. The Akita coat can absorb quite a bit of water and will decorate most of the wall and floor area of the average bathroom. In warm weather, the average pet can be allowed to air dry. In colder weather and for the show dog, blow drying may be necessary. For the show ring or for general appearances, the stand-off coat can be enhanced during the drying process. Use the pin brush to brush the hair toward the head as you dry. As well as enhancing the appearance of the coat it also will

This Akita pup doesn't seem too happy about having his nails cut. Acclimating your puppy to grooming procedures at a young age will make things easier when he is an adult.

help get air down into the coat. The furnishings on the legs are brushed back off the leg and the tail according to how it falls over the back and toward the tip.

As a finishing touch, trim the stray hairs on the furnishings and feet to appear neat. Unless you are an experienced groomer, consider using thinning shears as opposed to straight scissors or clippers. This will allow you to trim without giving the dog an obviously scissored look. For the show ring, whiskers are removed to "clean up the head." Clean ears and short nails are a must. While the hairs in front of the ear canal will catch most dirt and debris, the ears need to be

cleaned and checked regularly. In order to preserve the tight cat feet of the breed, regular and careful attention to nail clipping is required. Nails that are too long will cause the nails to splay and make the dog appear to be down in the pasterns as the foot is canted back to provide for excess nail length. The easiest way to keep the nails under control is a nail grinder. This is a breed whose nails cannot be too short.

It is extremely important that you start grooming the puppy as soon as it has settled into your home. A puppy who has been groomed regularly will grow into a more cooperative and pleasant adult.

FEEDING

Now let's talk about feeding your Akita, a subject so simple that it's amazing there is so much nonsense and misunderstanding about it. Is it expensive to feed a Akita? No, it is not! You can feed your Akita economically and keep him in perfect shape the year round, or you can feed him expensively. He'll thrive either way, and let's see why this is true.

First of all, remember an Akita is a dog. Dogs do not have a high degree of selectivity in their food, and unless you spoil them with great variety (and possibly turn them into poor, "picky" eaters) they will eat almost anything that they become accustomed to. Many dogs flatly refuse to eat nice, fresh beef. They pick around it and eat everything else. But meat—bah! Why? They aren't accustomed to it! They'd eat rabbit fast enough, but they refuse beef because they aren't used to it.

VARIETY NOT NECESSARY

A good general rule of thumb is forget all human preferences and don't give a thought to variety. Choose the right diet for your Akita and feed it to him day after day, year after year, winter and summer. But what is the right diet?

Hundreds of thousands of dollars have been spent in canine

Young puppies need to be fed three to four times a day in small quantities. Their food should be soaked in warm water in order to soften it so that it is easier to digest.

Some breeders recommend that you supplement your Akita's food with natural meats, vegetables, etc., while others prefer to use vitamin supplements that are available at pet shops.

nutrition research. The results are pretty conclusive, so you needn't go into a lot of experimenting with trials of this and that every other week. Research has proven just what your dog needs to eat and to keep healthy.

DOG FOOD

There are almost as many right diets as there are dog experts, but the basic diet most often recommended is one that consists of a dry food, either meal or kibble form. There are several of excellent quality, manufactured by reliable companies, research tested, and nationally advertised. They are inexpensive, highly satisfactory, and easily available in stores everywhere in containers of five to 50 pounds. Larger amounts cost less per pound, usually.

If you have a choice of brands, it is usually safer to choose the better known one; but even so, carefully read the analysis on the package. Do not choose any food in which the protein level is less than 25 percent, and be sure that this protein comes from both animal and vegetable sources. The good dog foods have meat meal, fish meal, liver, and such, plus protein from alfalfa and soy beans, as well as some dried-milk product. Note the vitamin content carefully. See that they are all there in good proportions; and be

Even though these Akita pups may not believe it, Nylafloss® is not a toy but rather a most effective agent in removing destructive plaque between the teeth and beneath the gumline where gum disease begins.

especially certain that the food contains properly high levels of vitamins A and D, two of the most perishable and important ones. Note the B-complex level, but don't worry about carbohydrate and mineral levels. These substances are plentiful and cheap and not likely to be lacking in a good brand.

The advice given for how to choose a dry food also applies to moist or canned types of dog foods, if you decide to feed one of these.

Having chosen a really good food, feed it to your Akita as the manufacturer directs. And once you've started, stick to it. Never change if you can possibly help it. A switch from one meal or kibble-type food can usually be made without too much upset; however, a change will almost invariably give you (and your Akita) some trouble.

It is best to put your dog on a feeding schedule. These Akita pups know exactly when it is time to eat and just where to find the food!

WHEN SUPPLEMENTS ARE NEEDED

Now what about supplements of various kinds, mineral and vitamin, or the various oils? They are all okay to add to your Akita's food. However, if you are feeding your Akita a correct diet, and this is easy to do, no supplements are necessary unless your Akita has been improperly fed, has been sick, or is having puppies. Vitamins and minerals are naturally present in all the foods; and to ensure against any loss through processing, they are added in concentrated form to the dog food you use. Except on the advice of your veterinarian, added amounts of vitamins can prove harmful to your Akita! The same risk goes with minerals.

FEEDING SCHEDULE

When and how much food to give your Akita? Most dogs do better if fed two or three smaller meals per day—this is not only better but vital to larger and deep-chested dogs. As to how to prepare the food and how much to give, it is generally best to follow the directions on the food package. Your own Akita may want a little more or a little less.

Fresh, cool water should always be available to your Akita. This is important to good health throughout his lifetime.

ALL AKITAS NEED TO CHEW

Puppies and young Akitas need something with resistance to chew on while their teeth and jaws are developing—for cutting the puppy teeth, to induce growth of the permanent teeth under the puppy teeth, to assist in getting rid of the puppy teeth at the proper time, to help the permanent teeth through the gums, to ensure normal jaw development, and to settle the permanent teeth solidly in the jaws.

The adult Akita's desire to chew stems from the instinct for tooth cleaning, gum massage, and jaw exercise—plus the need for an outlet for periodic doggie tensions.

This is why dogs, especially puppies and young dogs, will often destroy property worth hundreds of dollars when their chewing instincts are not diverted from their owners' possessions. And this is why you should provide your Akita with something to chew—something that has the necessary functional qualities, is desirable from the Akita's viewpoint, and is safe for him.

It is very important that your Akita not be permitted to chew on anything he can break or on any indigestible thing from which he can bite sizable chunks. Sharp pieces, such as from a bone which

Nothing can tear your Akita pup away from his Nylabone® chew toys. They are the most durable, safe, and economical answer to your Akita's chewing needs.

can be broken by a dog, may pierce the intestinal wall and kill. Indigestible things that can be bitten off in chunks, such as from shoes or rubber or plastic toys, may cause an intestinal stoppage (if not regurgitated) and bring painful death, unless surgery is promptly performed.

Strong natural bones, such as 4- to 8-inch lengths of round shin bone from mature beef—either the kind you can get from a butcher or one of the variety available commercially in pet stores—may serve your Akita's teething needs if his mouth is large enough to handle them effectively. You may be tempted to give your Akita puppy a smaller bone and he may not be able to break it when you do, but puppies grow rapidly and the power of their jaws constantly increases until maturity. This means that a growing Akita may break one of the smaller bones at any time, swallow the pieces, and die painfully before you realize what is wrong.

All hard natural bones are very abrasive. If your Akita is an avid chewer, natural bones may wear away his teeth prematurely; hence, they then should be taken away from your dog when the teething purposes have been

The Hercules™ by Nylabone® has been designed with strong jaws in mind. It is made of polyurethane, like car bumpers.

served. The badly worn, and usually painful, teeth of many mature dogs can be traced to excessive chewing on natural bones.

Contrary to popular belief, knuckle bones that can be chewed up and swallowed by your Akita provide little, if any, usable calcium or other nutriment. They do, however, disturb the digestion of most dogs and cause them to vomit the nourishing food they need.

Dried rawhide products of various types, shapes, sizes, and prices are available on the market and have become quite popular.

However, they don't serve the primary chewing functions very well; they are a bit messy when wet from mouthing, and most Akitas chew them up rather rapidly—but they have been considered safe for dogs until recently. Now, more and more incidents of death, and near death, by strangulation have been reported to be the results of partially swallowed chunks of rawhide swelling in the throat. More recently, some veterinarians have been attributing cases of acute constipation to large pieces of incompletely digested rawhide in the intestine.

A new product, molded rawhide, is very safe. During the process, the rawhide is melted and then injection molded into the familiar dog bone shape. It is very hard and is eagerly accepted by Akitas. The melting process also sterilizes the rawhide. Don't confuse this with pressed rawhide, which is nothing more than small strips of rawhide squeezed together.

The nylon bones, especially those with natural meat and bone fractions added, are probably the most complete, safe, and economical answer to the chewing need. Dogs cannot break them or bite off sizable chunks; hence, they are completely safe—and being longer lasting than other things offered for the purpose, they are economical.

Hard chewing raises little bristle-like projections on the surface of the nylon bones to provide effective interim tooth cleaning and vigorous gum massage, much in the same way your toothbrush does it for you. The little projections are raked off and swallowed in the form of thin shavings, but the chemistry of the nylon is such that they break down in the stomach fluids and pass through without effect.

The toughness of the nylon provides the strong chewing resistance needed for important jaw exercise and effectively aids teething functions, but there is no tooth wear because nylon is non-abrasive. Being inert, nylon does not support the growth of microorganisms; and it can be washed in soap and water or it can be sterilized by boiling or in an autoclave.

Nylabone® is highly recommended by veterinarians as a safe, healthy nylon bone that can't splinter or chip. Nylabone®

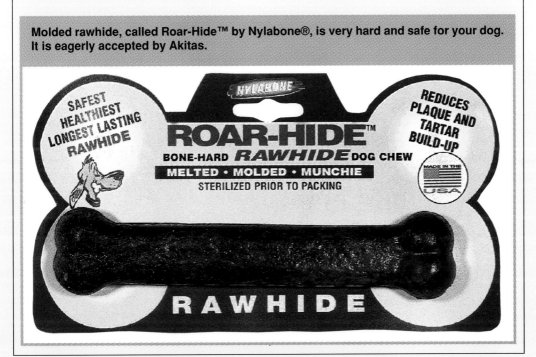

Molded rawhide, called Roar-Hide™ by Nylabone®, is very hard and safe for your dog. It is eagerly accepted by Akitas.

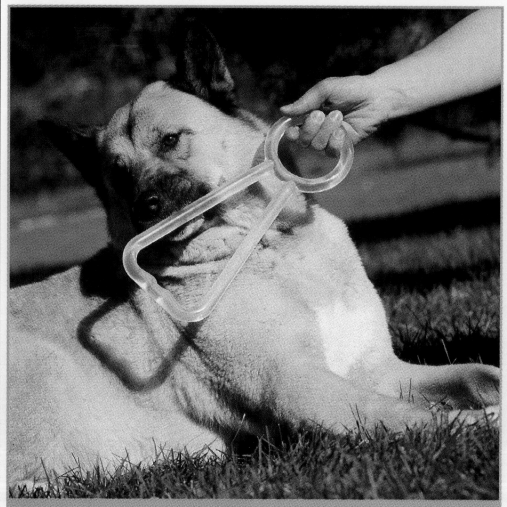

The Tug Toy by Gumabone® is a flavorful exercise device that can be enjoyed by both Akita and owner.

is frizzled by the dog's chewing action, creating a toothbrush-like surface that cleanses the teeth and massages the gums. Nylabone®, the only chew product made of flavor-impregnated solid nylon, is available in your local pet shop. Nylabone® is superior to the cheaper bones because it is made of virgin nylon, which is the strongest and longest-lasting type of nylon available. The cheaper bones are made from recycled or re-ground nylon scraps, and have a tendency to break apart and split easily.

Nothing, however, substitutes for periodic professional attention for your Akita's teeth and gums, not any more than your toothbrush can do that for you. Have your Akita's teeth cleaned at least once a year by your veterinarian (twice a year is better) and he will be happier, healthier, and far more pleasant to live with.

Gumabones® are best for teething puppies due to their softer composition. They come in a variety of shapes and colors and are available at your local pet shop.

TRAINING

You owe proper training to your Akita. The right and privilege of being trained is his birthright; and whether your Akita is going to be a handsome, well-mannered housedog and companion, a show dog, or whatever possible use he may be put to, the basic training is always the same—all must start with basic obedience, or what might be called "manner training."

Your Akita must come instantly when called and obey the "Sit" or "Down" command just as fast; he must walk quietly at "Heel," whether on or off lead. He must be mannerly and polite wherever he goes; he must be polite to strangers on the street and in stores. He must be mannerly in the presence of other dogs. He must not bark at children on roller skates, motorcycles, or other domestic animals. And he must be restrained from chasing cats. It is not a dog's inalienable right to chase cats, and he must be reprimanded for it.

A leash and collar are key pieces of equipment during the initial stages of your Akita's training. Once he is comfortable wearing these, obedience training will be a snap.

PROFESSIONAL TRAINING

How do you go about this training? Well, it's a very simple procedure, pretty well standardized by now. First, if you can afford the extra expense, you may send your Akita to a professional trainer, where in 30 to 60 days he will learn how to be a "good dog." If you enlist the services of a good professional trainer, follow his advice of when to come to see the dog. No, he won't forget you, but too-frequent visits at the wrong time may slow down his training progress. And using a "pro" trainer means that you will have to go for some training, too, after the trainer feels your Akita is ready to go home. You will have to learn how your Akita works, just what to expect of him and how to use what the dog has learned after he is home.

OBEDIENCE TRAINING CLASS

Another way to train your Akita (many experienced Akita people think this is the best) is to join an obedience training class right in your own community. There is such a group in nearly every community nowadays. Here you will be working with a group of people who are also just starting out. You will actually be training your own dog, since all work is done under the direction of a head trainer who will make suggestions to you and also tell you when and how to correct your Akita's errors. Then, too,

club or class in your locality. Sign up. Go to it regularly—every session! Go early and leave late! Both you and your Akita will benefit tremendously.

TRAIN HIM BY THE BOOK
The third way of training your

If you do not want your great big adult Akita to jump up on you or others, then you must not allow it when he is a cute little puppy. This type of behavior must be corrected at a young age.

working with such a group, your Akita will learn to get along with other dogs. And, what is more important, he will learn to do exactly what he is told to do, no matter how much confusion there is around him or how great the temptation is to go his own way.

Write to your national kennel club for the location of a training

Akita is by the book. Yes, you can do it this way and do a good job of it too. But in using the book method, select a book, buy it, study it carefully; then study it some more, until the procedures are almost second nature to you. Then start your training. But stay with the book and its advice and exercises. Don't start in and then make up a few rules of your

Successful Dog Training is one of the better books on dog training. The author, Michael Kamer, trains dogs for movie stars in Hollywood.

own. If you don't follow the book, you'll get into jams you can't get out of by yourself. If after a few hours of short training sessions your Akita is still not working as he should, get back to the book for a study session, because it's your fault, not the dog's! The procedures of dog training have been so well systemized that it must be your fault, since literally thousands of fine Akitas have been trained by the book.

After your Akita is "letter perfect" under all conditions, then, if you wish, go on to advanced training and trick work.

Your Akita will love his obedience training, and you'll burst with pride at the finished product! Your Akita will enjoy life even more, and you'll enjoy your Akita more. And remember—you *owe good training to your Akita.*

Your Akita puppy is like a clump of unmolded clay. It is up to you, the owner, to mold him into a well-mannered adult.

The Akita is generally good natured with children. However, it is imperative that children of all ages be taught how to properly handle the dog whether puppy or adult.

YOUR AKITA'S HEALTH

Akitas are generally healthy animals as are many working breeds. However, they are also subject to the genetic problems associated with size. These include sporadic growing pains and hip dysplasia.

Puppies, during strong growth spurts, will occasionally limp on one leg or another. However, the malformation or improper seating of the hip into the socket is a genetic defect. This is a polygenetic problem that can carry from generation to generation. Dogs not certified as free of hip dysplasia by either the Orthopedic Foundation for

Animals (OFA) or the International Canine Genetics (ICG) PennHip™ program should not be bred. Current American Kennel Club registrations will carry the OFA numbers of certified dogs. Owners also receive certificates from OFA attesting to the fact the dog has passed the hip x-ray evaluation.

Another prevalent genetic problem in Akitas is hypothyroidism. This is a low or underactive thyroid. A number of physical traits are indicative of possible thyroid problems in an otherwise healthy animal. They include a poor quality of sparse coat, sporadic or nonexistent estrous cycles in the female, and some temperament problems that cannot be traced to other hereditary or environmental factors. All are good reasons to have a simple blood test to determine thyroid activity. Treatment for the condition is a pill a day for the rest of the dog's life. Dogs affected by hypothyroidism should not be bred; however, considering the number of Akitas affected, many are bred despite the condition.

Akitas are also subject to progressive retinal atrophy (PRA) that causes blindness. While the condition may not surface until later in the dog's life, the eyes should be checked annually, especially if the dog is being bred. Breeders should also be aware of a condition known as micro-opthalmia, where the eye socket is too large for the eyeball.

The best book on dog health is *The Owner's Guide to Dog Health* by Dr. Lowell Ackerman. It is available at your local pet shop.

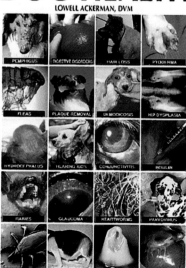

Akitas are generally healthy animals, as are many working breeds. However, they are also subject to the genetic problems associated with size.

ACTIVITIES FOR THE AKITA

The Akita has proven its adaptability to the demands of modern society. He has proven to be quite versatile and there are many activities in which you and your dog can participate.

Because of the Akita's history as a fighting breed, the early breed fanciers and parent clubs encouraged obedience training. It is still very important that you always present your Akita in a positive light. In recent years, communities looking to pass vicious dog legislation and/or breed bans have looked more closely than the fancy would like at the breed. While the Akita has not yet been banned anywhere in the United States, it only takes one incident to cause a problem for the whole breed. Thus obedience training and Canine Good Citizenship certification are becoming more and more important, particularly in the case of the working breed types.

While Akitas are not the best breed for regimented competition, they do learn and make quite respectable social canines. Their intelligence and independent nature may make the training more challenging than some other breeds, but they are willing to please and will work with you as a team providing you are patient. They are relatively calm and quiet, and well-socialized Akitas will adjust to the group exercises quite readily. Their protective nature can be controlled and properly directed through training and should not be a deterrence to participation in most events.

Note that the breed usually learns quickly and prefers shorter training sessions. Over-training the highly intelligent dog will often result in a bored and uncooperative animal. However, most training problems can be avoided by starting the Akita at a young age. An enthusiastic puppy is much easier to get under control than a hundred pounds of misbehaving muscle.

A more recent activity that requires minimal obedience training is the Canine Good Citizenship program. Certification under this program is highly recommended for all working type breeds and has, in some areas, been accepted as proof of the soundness of a dog's temperament.

Akitas have also excelled in agility training and competition. Dogs that are structurally sound should adapt easily. They have the athletic ability, all they need is an enthusiastic owner.

Weight pulling is another activity for which the Akita is built. It is also a great way to keep your dog in top condition. A side step further and dog sledding is not beyond the ability of the breed. While Schutzhund, French Ring Sport, and hunting have fallen into disfavor with the organized fancy, they are still valid activities in which Akitas have participated successfully.

An Akita heeling on a leash in novice obedience. Although Akitas are more challenging to train than some other breeds, they are willing to please and will work well as a team with their owners.

Although there are many organized activities for your Akita, the best activity is playtime with you. This Akita and owner are enjoying a winter wonderland.

Ch. The Widow-Maker O'BJ, with owner-breeder-handler Barbara J. Andrews. The Widow-Maker is undoubtedly the most famous Akita in America and is the winner of ten Best in Show awards and is the #2 sire of all time.

SHOWING YOUR AKITA

A show Akita is a comparatively rare thing. He is one out of several litters of puppies. He happens to be born with a degree of physical perfection that closely approximates the standard by which the breed is judged in the show ring. Such a dog should, on maturity, be able to win or approach his championship in good, fast company at the larger shows. Upon finishing his championship, he is apt to be as highly desirable as a breeding animal. As a proven stud, he will automatically command a high price for service.

Showing Akitas is a lot of fun—yes, but it is a highly competitive sport. While all the experts were once beginners, the odds are against a novice. You will be showing against experienced handlers, often people who have devoted a lifetime to breeding, picking the right ones, and then showing those dogs through to their championships. Moreover, the most perfect Akita ever born has faults, and in your hands the faults will be far more evident than with the experienced handler who knows how to minimize his Akita's faults. These are but a few points on the sad side of the picture.

The experienced handler, as I say, was not born knowing the ropes. He learned—*and so can you!* You can if you will put in the same time, study and keen observation that he did. But it will take time!

KEY TO SUCCESS

First, search for a truly fine show prospect. Take the puppy home, raise him by the book, and

Ch. Overhill's Cherokee Lite Fut, breeder-owner-handled by Ms. Meg Purnell-Carpenter, demonstrates correct movement in the ring.

Ch. Kinouk's A Piece of Work, bred and owned by Joan Harper Young, being baited in the ring. Conformation showing is hard work for both dog and handler.

as carefully as you know how, give him every chance to mature into the Akita you hoped for. My advice is to keep your dog out of big shows, even Puppy Classes, until he is mature. Maturity in the male is roughly two years; with the female, 14 months or so. When your Akita is approaching maturity, start out at match shows, and, with this experience for both of you, then go gunning for the big wins at the big shows.

Next step, read the standard by which the Akita is judged. Study it until you know it by heart. Having done this, and while your puppy is at home (where he should be) growing into a normal, healthy Akita, go to every dog show you can possibly reach. Sit at the ringside and watch Akita judging. Keep your ears and eyes open. Do your own judging, holding each of those dogs against the standard, which you now know by heart.

In your evaluations, don't start looking for faults. Look for the virtues—the best qualities. How does a given Akita shape up against the standard? Having looked for and noted the virtues, then note the faults and see what prevents a given Akita from standing correctly or moving well. Weigh these faults against the virtues, since, ideally, every feature of the dog should contribute to the harmonious whole dog.

"RINGSIDE JUDGING"

It's a good practice to make notes on each Akita, always

Every year a full-color book is published with portraits of all the great champion dogs who win at the Westminster Kennel Club, including the Akita. This book is not expensive and is a MUST if you plan on showing your Akita.

holding the dog against the standard. In "ringside judging," forget your personal preference for this or that feature. What does the standard say about it? Watch carefully as the judge places the dogs in a given class. It is difficult from the ringside always to see why number one was placed over the second dog. Try to follow the judge's reasoning. Later try to talk with the judge after he is finished. Ask him questions as to why he placed certain Akitas and not others. Listen while the judge explains his placings, and, I'll say right here, any judge worthy of his license should be able to give reasons.

When you're not at the ringside, talk with the fanciers and breeders who have Akitas. Don't be afraid to ask opinions or say that you don't know. You have a lot of listening to do, and it will help you a great deal and speed up your personal progress if you are a good listener.

THE NATIONAL CLUB

You will find it worthwhile to join the national Akita club and to subscribe to its magazine. From the national club, you will learn the location of an approved regional club near you. Now, when your young Akita is eight to ten months old, find out the dates of match shows in your section of the country. These differ from regular shows only in that no championship points are given. These shows are especially designed to launch young dogs (and new handlers) on show careers.

Ch. The Joker is Wild O'BJ handled by former owner Roger Kaplan. Joker, one of the top Akita show dogs of our time, is a best in show winner bred by B.J. Andrews.

ENTER MATCH SHOWS

With the ring deportment you have watched at big shows firmly in mind and practice, enter your Akita in as many match shows as you can. When in the ring, you have two jobs. One is to see to it that your Akita is always being seen to its best advantage. The other job is to keep your eye on the judge to see what he may want you to do next. Watch only the judge and your Akita. Be quick and be alert; do exactly as the judge directs. Don't speak to him except to answer his questions. If he does something you don't like, don't say so. And don't irritate the judge (and everybody else) by constantly talking and fussing with your dog.

In moving about the ring, remember to keep clear of dogs beside you or in front of you. It is my advice to you *not* to show your Akita in a regular point show until he is at least close to maturity and after both you and your dog have had time to perfect ring manners and poise in the match shows.

SUGGESTED READING

OTHER BOOKS ON THE AKITA

A fascinating story unfolds as you skim through the pages of this beautifully illustrated volume, *The Book of the Akita(H-1075)* by Joan McDonald Brearley. Akita lovers everywhere will find invaluable information about their beloved

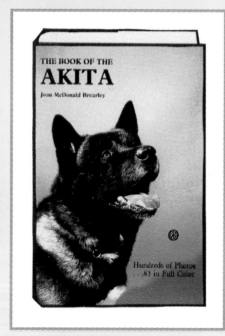

H-1075

breed in this book as the author traces the history and development of Akitas in Japan, The United States, and other parts of the world. The book features hundreds of photographs, 83 of which are in color. Everything Akita owners need to know about how to select and care for their dogs is included here.

The World of the Akita(TS-256) by Barbara J. Andrews is the most comprehensive and colorful book on the breed ever published.

Barbara J. Andrews, known as "BJ" to the Akita fancy, is the most successful breeder of Akitas in the world, having bred approximately 200 champions internationally. Over 400 pages in length, *The World of the Akita* contains hundreds of color photographs of the the great champions, dams, and sires as well as detailed chapters on the origin of the Akita in Japan and the United States, the breed standard, Akita temperament and trainability, breeding, whelping and caring for puppies, showing, obedience, and general maintenance. The author, who is the originator of the Register of Merit system accepted by the Akita Club of America, introduces in this book the Akita Hall of Fame, including the names and photographs of the country's top dogs and breeders. Indispensable and definitive, this volume is absolutely breathtaking, as well as fascinating and challenging— just like the Akita dog himself!

GENERAL DOG BOOKS

The following books are all published by T.F.H. Publications, Inc. and are recommended to you for additional information:

The Atlas of Dog Breeds of the World (H-1091) by Bonnie Wilcox, DVM and Chris Walkowicz traces the history and highlights the characteristics, appearance and function of every recognized dog breed in the world. 409 different breeds receive full-color treatment and individual study. Hundreds of breeds in addition to those recognized by the American Kennel Club and the Kennel Club of Great Britain are included—the dogs of the world complete! The ultimate reference work, comprehensive

H-1091

dog person. It is the most complete single volume on the dog ever published, covering more breeds than any other book as well as other relevant topics, including health, showing, training, breeding, anatomy, veterinary terms, and much more. No dog book before has ever offered this many stunning color photographs of all breeds, dog sports, and topics (over 1300 in full color).

A very successful spin-off of the *Atlas* is *The Mini-Atlas of Dog Breeds* (H-1106), written by Andrew DePrisco and James B. Johnson. This compact but comprehensive book has been praised and recommended by most national dog publications for its utility and reader-friendliness. The true field guide for dog lovers.

TS-175

coverage, intelligent and delightful discussions. The perfect gift book.

***THE MOST COMPLETE DOG BOOK EVER PUBLISHED: A CANINE LEXICON* (TS-175)**
by Andrew DePrisco and James Johnson, is an up-to-date encyclopedic dictionary for the

H-1106

Teaching the family dog has never been more fun and easy! *Just Say "Good Dog"* (TS-204) is a new approach in teaching dogs to be good family dogs and good house dogs. This most original manual to canine education by Linda Goodman, author and dog teacher, addresses all the basic commands and day-to-day problems as well as the considerations and responsibilities of dog ownership. Living with a dog should be a rewarding experience, and this book will show you how. Delightful illustrations by AnnMarie Freda accompany the author's fun and anecdotal text to reinforce the importance of a positive approach to dog training. *Just Say "Good Dog"* is both very informative and authoritative, as the author, assisted by Marlene Trunnell, offers many years of experience and know-how.

TS-204

Everybody Can Train Their Own Dog (TW-113) by Angela White is a fabulous reference guide for all dog owners. This well written, easy-to-understand book covers all training topics in alphabetical order for instant location. In addition to teaching, this book provides problem solving and problem prevention techniques that are fundamental to training. All teaching methods are based on motivation and kindness, which bring out the best of a dog's natural ability and instinct.

TW-113